240

PEWTER

The Candlestick Maker's Bawle

'A Family Portrait'

Edward Burnworth in Newgate Prison, April 1726.
From: *The Lives of the Most Remarkable Criminals.*

PEWTER
The Candlestick Maker's Bawle

'A Family Portrait'

KENNETH G. GORDON

Published by the author, 28 Cumberland Road, Congleton, Cheshire CW12 4PH
and printed by Gee & Son (Denbigh) Ltd., Chapel Street, Denbigh, Clwyd.

IN LOVING AND TREASURED MEMORY

OF

MY VERY SPECIAL DAUGHTER

WENDY

ॐ

PAMIĘCI MOJEJ UKOCHANEJ

I

NIGDY NIEZAPMOMNIANEJ

WYJĄTKOWEJ CÓRKI

WENDY

CONTENTS

FOREWORD

The Worshipful Company of Pewterers is indebted to the members of the Pewter Society for the detailed work they have carried out on our extensive records spanning over 500 years.

Ken Gordon's research on ball knopped candlesticks, provides us with the first analysis of the range of styles that were produced and how they may be tentatively dated by a careful comparison of the known surviving examples. It is a most important addition to our knowledge of what we now believe was a common item of household ware, widely used in England in the 17th and early 18th centuries.

Let us hope that this valuable work will result in more of these interesting pieces being brought to our attention and their being given the due recognition that they surely deserve.

CHARLES HULL

Master of the Worshipful Company of Pewterers
1992 - 1993

THE PHOTOGRAPHER

It has been my pleasure to assist Ken Gordon in the production of his unique study on pewter ball-knop candlesticks. Throughout the book I have maintained a certain style of photography, resulting in an easy visual flow of material, to enhance the candlesticks. The majority of photographs has been taken on location over a substantial period of time and under varying conditions, usually far from ideal. Maintaining visual consistency was not easily achieved.

I would like to thank the Directors, Curators, Technicians and Photographers within the public bodies who permitted me to take the photographs for this book and, above all, Ken Gordon for allowing me the privilege of illustrating his book.

JAMES JOHNSON
St. Albans, 9 August 1993

ACKNOWLEDGEMENTS

Sincerest thanks are expressed to all the undermentioned for their assistance, kindness and whole hearted co-operation in the production of this work.

Mr. and Mrs. M. Arnold	Dr. A. S. Law
Mr. and Mrs. L. Bonner	Mr. D. Little
Mr. N. Brazell	Mr. J. H. Myrtle
Mr. W. Buckell	Mr. A. R. Neish
A private collector in the USA	Dr. I. D. Robinson
Dr. J. Hatcher	Mr. A. J. Russell
Dr. R. F. Homer	Mr. S. Shemmell
Mr. P. Hornsby	Mr. and Mrs. M. Toothill
Mr. J. Johnson	Mrs. J. Gotabeck-Klimczak
Mr. P. Kidd	Mr. and Mrs. M. Walker

The National Trust Arlington Court (Mr. J. Stoute)
Cheltenham Art Gallery and Museums (Mrs. M. Greenstead)
The Fitzwilliam Museum Cambridge (Mr. S. Jervis and M/s J. Poole)
The Hunterian Museum and Art Gallery (Dr. L. Keppie and Miss A. Nesbitt)
The New South Wales Art Gallery
The Victoria and Albert Museum (Mr. A. North)
The Colonial Williamsburg Foundation (Mr. G. Hood and Mr. J. Davis)
Messrs. Gee and Son (Denbigh) Ltd. (Mr. T. Alun Williams)

The motivation for the writing and production of this book is readily apparent from the dedication on the front page and upon this I will not dwell further than to say that other considerations have intruded since the idea first came to me. Personal financial gain has no part to play in the publication of this work and indeed it is difficult to imagine anyone of sound mind endeavouring to capitalise on a production devoted to such a limited field and hence a limited readership. However it is hoped that the book will help to fill a gap in a largely ignored aspect of the pewtering genre and I find myself almost unwittingly offering it to the Pewter Society and all its members and camp followers for the untold interest and pleasure I have derived over the years from the Society's existence and the friendship of its members.

Whilst a list of acknowledgements appears later may I pay special tribute to the organisations, museums etc and private persons, many of them Society members, who have co-operated so willingly and generously with their time and effort and have allowed the loan of specimens or photographs for use in the book.

Experience suggests that an overlong preface ensures the certainty that it will be ignored and I will keep this one short. In the Society's Journal of Autumn 1981 my article entitled 'The Candlestick Maker's Bawle' indicated that I had fallen hook, line and sinker for the challenge presented by the late Christopher Peal's observation in his 'British Pewter' — 'exactly where the ball knop fits in is not known for certain'. The present publication is a progression of my article and although there are perhaps only some fifty or so British Ball Knopped Candlesticks in existence at this time, it does suggest that even that number having survived so long is an indication that hundreds more of the style were originally made, albeit in several forms. Following upon my first article, I have incorporated into this book all the material I have been able to harvest in support of the series of admirable photographs taken by my friend Mr. James Johnson, whose energy, resource and professionalism have resulted in this book being a much grander publication than was originally envisaged. These photographs depict all the readily accessible candlesticks of the British Ball-knop type and should prove invaluable as a fairly comprehensive record of what has existed when the owners and perhaps the specimens have passed on. Any specimens emerging after this publication will have to be the subject of a separate work and I am well aware that several have slipped through the net and into temporary oblivion.

Special thanks then to James Johnson and also to Dr. 'Sandy' Law for his editing, proof reading and assistance in providing important information on early pewtering and pewterers, but particularly for his decision to transfer from his collection to mine a specimen of the British Ball knop which appears amongst the photographs in this book. In these special acknowledgements, it is essential to make mention of my good friend Mr. Stanley Shemmell. His unique ability sympathetically to restore and enhance early pewter led to his discovery of the ownership intials 'GH' common to the plate, dome lid tankard and ball knop candlestick displayed at the front of this book. On behalf of both the Church and private collectors, Stanley has devoted much time, effort and pewtering skill, but as a fortuitous example of his talent I rank this piece of detection as a particularly outstanding achievement.

Lastly may I offer to the Worshipful Company of Pewterers on behalf of the Society and myself, special appreciation for its hospitality and unfailing courtesy over the years and sincerest good wishes for their continuing presence as a symbol of stability in a changing world. It is hoped that the Company will accept a copy of this publication as a token of the special esteem in which it is held.

K. G. GORDON   *5th November, 1991*

CANDLESTICK MAKER'S BAWLE — A FAMILY PORTRAIT

INTRODUCTION

The pewter ball-knopped candlestick has been in little favour with those dabbling in the pewter scene over the years and as the Master of the Worshipful Company of Pewterers has been kind enough to write a foreword in endorsement of this book, I trust he will think no ill of me if I comment that, so far as I am aware, the Company does not have a ball knop candlestick in its fine and otherwise unrivalled collection.

At the outset of my acquaintanceship with the Pewter Society more than 20 years ago, vague and unsubstantiated rumblings amongst its members led one to believe that the ball-knopped candlestick had some Continental influences. For purposes of comparison with what is believed to be the truly British ball knopped candlestick, there will be found towards the end of this book some references to photographs and examples of the Continental ball knops. Because their origins appear to be based entirely in the United Kingdom, the photographs of our British ball knops appear at the forefront of the book and on the comparisons between the two my case rests. The Continental ball knops appear unrepentantly Continental and none the worse for that. By the same token, the unobtrusive simplicity or compatibility with other pewterware of the seventeenth and early eighteenth centuries are the markers for the British made candlesticks.

In 'The Connoisseur' of April 1956, A. V. Sutherland-Graeme in an article entitled 'Seventeenth Century Pewter Candlesticks' writes 'I am aware that some consider that all these more ornate examples (of candlesticks) are of continental origin, for the reasons:

    i)   That they exhibit to some extent the characteristics of those early candlesticks mentioned in the first part of this article and

    ii)   that none of them is marked.

As regards the first point, I do not consider that much weight attaches to it. Something like three quarters of a century divides them, and fine craftmanship was general all over Europe in the seventeenth century. As to the second point, I would say that far too few of these ornate examples exist (even supposing them all to be genuine) to enable one to be dogmatic. On the other hand, perhaps twenty or thirty times as many English Communion Flagons of the first quarter of the seventeenth century exist, hardly any of which is marked. But their nationality has never been challenged: moreover continental pieces of this period are frequently found to be marked several times with ornate touches, so that from both points of view I do not think the argument holds water.' (end of quote)

So far as one can ascertain, it would seem that Sutherland-Graeme was challenging an assertion made by H. H. Cotterell that the Genesis of the English Domestic Pewter Candlestick could be ascribed to Holland. It would seem that out of this acorn grew the oak tree that ball-knops were continental, whether ornate or otherwise. It is obviously necessary, if one is so minded, to read all of Sutherland-Graeme's article, but the gist of the comments is that the anecdotes arising from remarks taken out of context by Howard Cotterell have led to misapprehensions by those not inclined to make their own judgement. Some of our British ball knops (not too many) have now made their homes in other countries and are brightening the lives of others on distant shores. This book containing the excellent photographs by James Johnson will help to complement the scene both home and away.

To avoid any misunderstandings, the writer in the context of this publication defines the ball-knopped candlestick as the simple, tubular stemmed construction with a single round or flattened ball or similar protuberance on the lower half or middle of the stem. Anything departing from this description does not come within the scope of this study and a glance through the illustrations will clearly outline the type under discussion.

In the eyes of some, the *gadrooned* ball-knop candlestick is perhaps the most desirable specimen in its field, but I have referred in the title of this book to the family of ball knops and such it is, having developed from the less sophisticated pieces of the early 17th century and possibly earlier. This family, ugly ducklings or swans is approaching extinction and all must be considered of equal historical value.

CHAPTER ONE

STRUCTURE OF THE BALL KNOP

The ball knop is from observations and research constructed of six or sometimes seven pieces. From those examined and depicted in this book, the structural features are as follows:—

1. *The nozzle flange* — was circular when manufactured and diameters vary, the stem flange being vestigial when associated with a removeable sconce but considerable, indeed even up to 4 inches in diameter, on the removeable sconce itself. Integrated sconces on the other hand have more modest flanges usually from one and a half to about two inches in width. Amongst the specimens depicted here it will be noted that one flange has been restored and has a square, rounded corner replacement, whilst a second has had the flange removed entirely.

2. *The stem* — often composed of one, but sometimes two segments, usually having an applied reeding or marked by turned circles, often referred to here as a fillet.

3. *The nozzle plate* — consists of a circular, flat disc part way down the stem. One of the examples examined has a seven pointed 'asterisk' type mark on the underside of the disc. (See reference to Cancellation Marks in the Journal of the Pewter Society Spring 1982 and Autumn 1982) — probably irrelevant, but worth a mention.

4. *The Ball* — cast in upper and lower segments, the later examples having a fillet surrounding the join, in addition to which some have gadrooned ornamentation decorating both segments.

5. *The base* — may be round and trumpet shaped, round and dished or recessed, octangular and dished or octangular rising to a plinth before meeting the lower segment of the ball. Bases may be decorated with gadrooning or with a 'chattered tooling' effect, but quite frequently are without ornamentation. It would seem that the earlier ball knops had a quite significantly wide flange surrounding the circular bases. The plinth and pedestal are of course the lower stages of the candlestick between the bottom section of the ball and the base.

Simplicity of line, probably in many cases to facilitate workmanship, was one of the earlier features of the ball knops, but their no-nonsense, 'smokestack' characteristics provide, a large measure of their workaday charm, whilst the gadrooning of the twenty years or so of the late 17th and early 18th centuries is a delightful decoration, which has probably assisted in the preservation of pieces so decorated. The plain styles are in comparison to overall original production numbers, now probably much the rarer.

CHAPTER TWO

DATING THE BALL-KNOP

Quoted, possibly to distraction, in other publications are extracts from the records of the Worshipful Company of Pewterers of 1612-13 as portrayed in Welch's History of the Company. For the convenience of the reader and without apology, part of the extract relating to matters only relevant to this study are once again reproduced hereunder.

'A meetinge (27th February) be pore mr dcor wood maistr of or company and mr John Cowdewell warden; of certen tryffeleres for the Syzeing of wares, Vizt. Chosen for that purpose.

1. Mr. Hughe Newton
2. Mr. Thomas Parratt
3. Mr. Geo: Smyther
4. Mr. Gabr. Butcher
5. Mr. Henr: Glover
6. Mr. Edwd Glover
7. Mr. Wm Hylle
8. Mr. Wm Hatfeild
9. Wm Rydge
10. Wm Granger
11. James Jones
12. John Goodwyn

Att whch tyme was Syzed by them theis seuall pcells of Tryffles as followe vizt:

		II		
Ould fashion	Ordinarie highe candlesticks to weighe by peare	03	0	qrtr
candlesticks	Greate middle p pae	02	0	di
	Greate pyller p pae	03	00	
	Smale middle p pae	02	di	qrtr
	Middle pyller p pae	02 di	00	
Geo.	Greate new fashion p pae	03	00	
Smythe	Smale fashion p pae	02 di	00	
	Great bell p pae	03 di	00	
	Lowe bell p pae	02	00	
	Greate wryteinge p pae	01 di	00	
	Midd wryteing p pae	01	00	
	Smale wryteing p pae	00	3	qr
Candlesticks	Grawnd p pae	04 di	00	
with	Ordinarie highe p pae	03	0	qrtr
bawles	Greate middle p pae	02	0	di
	Smale middle p pae	02	0	qrtr
	Great wryteing p pae	01	0	di

From this assay it can be deduced that candlesticks were made of trifle metal and by inference that had 'candlesticks with bawles' been old fashioned in 1612-1613 they would doubtless have appeared under the 'Ould Fashion Candlesticks' heading. The assay also illustrates the emphasis, often overlooked, which was placed by the Pewterers Company on the weights of their wares. At some stage, this factor may prove of help in establishing ages or identities of certain pewter items.

Trifle or Tryffle is described in Welsh's History as an alloy of 82 parts of tin to 18 parts antimony. Other definitions may no doubt exist.

One of the tryffeleres Mr. Geo Smyther, chosen to assist in the assay or syzeing of wares is presumably the Geo Smythe privileged to have his name in the margin opposite to 'Greate new fashion' etc for some reason not readily apparent. It is possible to speculate, probably quite accurately, upon this, but how tantalising it is not to *know* what George Smythe produced. There is nothing which comes readily to mind in the way of 'new fashion' candlesticks, which one could suggest is eligible for inclusion in this category. There is no clue and we must be grateful for such records as we have.

The syzeing, however, is the first reasonable plank in the family tree of ball-knop dating and whilst no evidence of a ball-knop of this early period, contemporaneous with the assay has emerged, some evidence exists of what the ball-knop looked like some thirty odd years later. The weight referred to in the syzeing has some relevance to one of the candlesticks depicted later and it is perhaps reasonable to assume that so far as this type is concerned, they were little different. Indeed, we have grounds for associating Gabriel Butcher one of the tryffelers engaged in the syzeing, with the maker of the said candlestick.

Dating the ball-knop presents the researcher with problems. Only a small number now bear a maker's touch, which appears to have been applied exclusively to that most vulnerable of positions for a candlestick namely, the flange. A close scrutiny and a 'Brillo' pad can sometimes bring a touch into the light of day. It is a fact that none of the ball knop candlesticks examined to date have any touch mark *other* than on the flange, although ownership marks can often be seen there and on the under side of the base.

Having found a touch, the difficulty of attributing it to a maker is hampered by the fact that it may be pre-touch plate, provincial and probably not recorded anywhere, or so at variance with a maker's larger touch as to be unattributable.

So much for touches then. A search for contemporary paintings depicting the ball knop has yielded nothing to assist in dating and I am reliably informed by my associates versed in silver styles that there is no known indication of the ball knop having been made in silver although there are known examples in brass, sadly without positive aids to dating. In relation to the ball knop candlesticks illustrated in this book, a number of attractive ones exist with the octagonal sided bases akin to silver styles where the octagonal appearance is created by a square minus corners base, which is described as octangular as a more concise description of a base with four long sides and four short ones. The octagonal style described by Randle Holme in 1649 is unlikely to have been of this ilk, it being perhaps more likely that the type to which he refers had the equal sided octagonal base. Cripps in 'Old English Plate' refers to 'square minus corners' base candlesticks in the time of Charles II and William and Mary which were made in silver. Referring to bases of the type in silver candlesticks, Alexander O. Curle describes the earliest dateable to 1686 and depicts one of rather similar base as late as 1740 in a paper on Domestic Candlesticks from the Fourteenth to the Eighteenth Century in the 'Proceedings of the Society of Antiquaries of Scotland'.

In a rather unlikely source, namely 'Lives of the Most Remarkable Criminals' edited by Arthur L. Hayward is a print from the Newgate Calendar entitled 'A Prisoner under Pressure in Newgate'. Above an unfortunate prisoner Edward Burnworth, who is said to have carried weights of 424 lbs on his chest before consenting to plead, stands a man holding in his left hand what to all intents and purposes is a ball knopped trumpet-based candlestick. The date of this event is put at April 1726!

This later than the generally accepted date for ball knops is in some degree corroborated by a piece of pewter in my collection, viz: a 4½ins diameter trumpet-based footed paten, bearing the touch of E. Fairbrother 1723. The base diameter is similar to the base of a candlestick shown in this book, to which I attribute a similar dating. The 'trumpet' is connected to the paten base by an appendage which with minor adaptation could form the lower half of a ball knop.

E. Fairbrother is referred to in Cotterell's 'Old Pewter — Its Makers and Marks' as being of Lancaster or Knutsford — 1723 to 1750, but this name is again shown in R. J. A. Shelley's List of Wigan and Liverpool Pewterers as follows:—

> Fairbrother Edward I flourished 1680-1727
> Fairbrother Edward II occurs 1756

Make of this what you will, there are reasonable grounds for believing that in the north west of England at least, the trumpet base was still in vogue in the 1720s.

Having commented on the range of dating so far known of the pewter ball knop candlestick, it is perhaps worthy of comment that the well known early 12th century Gloucester candlestick of gilt bell metal (which may have been made in England) and a number of bronze candlesticks of the 13th century were made in the ball knop style as was some glass ware of the 16th century and c1700. This seems consistent with the view that the ball knop candlestick in pewter was part of a family of an accepted style and not as has been stated by some, a modification of this or that, developing along with improvements in candle wax etc. It is a personal view that the ball protuberance was not only a means of convenience for carrying the candlestick, but also assisted in dissipating the heat of the lighted candle in the descent of the flame down its length and therefore an early form of insulation. With the disappearance of the ball knop in the 18th century, it would seem that the chamberstick with its ringed handle and drip tray became popular and indeed no pewter chambersticks of the 17th century are known to the writer, although it is understood they were made in silver at the end of that century.

Further aids to dating the ball knop candlestick, whilst based on judgement, gut feelings and experience of examination of similar specimens, are within the province of all of us and are not sculptured in stone. It is on some of these facets, that the observations contained in parts of this book are based. The book in other words is purely an airing of views taking into account my own research, judgement and prejudices. The reader reads and makes his own choices.

Included in these observations are the following : —

1. A ball knop candlestick with removeable sconce is quite likely to relate to the first half of the 17th century.
2. Broader stem fillets are likely to proximate to the pre-1660 period of the 17th century.
3. Plain unfilleted balls again seem to occur more frequently in the earlier 17th century pieces.
4. Gadrooned decoration and octangular bases appear to predominate, though not exclusively so, in the 1680 to 1715 period by association with styles in other types of ware.
5. A dished base and outer flange may be a sign of an early piece, but a dished base may on some evidence suggest manufacture in Bristol or its environs. See photograph captions where appropriate.
6. A vertical seamed stem or other features including good, poor or crude condition can be evidence of provincial or manufacturing peculiarities and whilst it may be, does not have to be an indication of the age of a piece. It should be said that the writer is only aware of the possible existence of one specimen of vertical seaming of the stem. This publication does not illustrate that particular example.

7. Roll top, or bent down flanges appear in general to be a modification to a candlestick to allow the shedding of extra light as the candle diminishes in size. There are only to my knowledge a very few instances of a down-sloping flange having been manufactured in that form on ball-knop candlesticks. The mention of the detachable nozzle as a 'prolonger' in 17th century records and the very reference in the Company records of candlesticks 'wryteing' are evidence of items being purpose-built for both economy and utility and for those without the finance or motivation to purchase the purpose-built, improvisation was the answer. Anecdotal and 'granny' tales to the contrary, seem unconvincing.

8. Perhaps conversely, candlesticks with recessed or dished bases appear mainly to have been manufactured in that form, rather than the minority which had the plinth physically depressed into a drip tray based conversion.

9. Weighing of the ball knop candlesticks to which I have had access may provide some assistance in reconciling the 1612-1613 assay with certain of the ball knops still surviving, but absence or omission of records may have conspired along with other factors to make a greater affinity so far impracticable. However, the avoirdupois weights are now available for posterity, awaiting the outcome of further researches. A separate chapter on weights is included.

As an out and out reactionary, it has given the writer some pleasure to avoid any reference to the metric system but in any event the cerebral gymnastics involved in the previously mentioned weight conversion exercises have been generally inconclusive and sufficiently strenuous to tax the patience of the writer and all concerned to the utmost. In brief therefore, our family of pewter British ball-knops may for the present (a back door must be left open for future discoveries or developments), be dated from about 1610 to about 1730, with many of our present survivors having been made between c1680 and c1715. This harlequin troop, consisting of s ophisticates and plebeians manufactured between the latter dates are obliged to have their dating open-ended awaiting developments in the future.

No matter how hard one tries, the future will often confound the best analysis and hypothesis and despite the best endeavours of a writer to maintain the integrity of his work, the lurking snake in the grass will no doubt bite him in the ankle sooner or later. For these reasons as many escape routes as possible have been left, consistent with saying anything at all. A glance at the next chapter on Weights will confirm this.

CHAPTER THREE

WEIGHTS

At each end of the golfing spectrum exist tigers and rabbits. Despite the efforts of tutors long gone, the writer has always been and will no doubt remain a mathematical rabbit. It is thus unwise to indulge one's ignorance in a publication devoted to a serious attempt at historical research. However, the 1612-13 Assay referred to earlier, displays quite conspicuously the importance the Pewterers Company attached to the weights of their wares. It is not therefore possible to ignore the matter in our discussion on Candlesticks with 'bawles' and the nettle has to be grasped. All the candlesticks photographed by James Johnson and seen by myself have therefore been weighed, possibly with some lack of strict accuracy, but nevertheless weighed, on avoirdupois scales.

At the outset it has to be said that nothing seems to match particularly well with our avoirdupois weights and those weights given in the Assay and whilst it is perhaps unkind to suggest it, there may have been more mathematical rabbits than tigers in the Worshipful Company of Pewterers. One reason for this observation may be seen in Mr. Welch's History of the Worshipful Company of Pewterers, where a record of 1729-30 refers to:

> 'Mr. Warden Eden laid (6th August) before the Court a Table made by Mr. James Nicholson Shewing what Quantity of Tin being melted and mixed with one Pound of Lead increaseth the Weight of the Cast from the Hall Essay Moulds by one Grain to ffifty five'

Then follows the Table of Weights. The record goes on to express the thanks of the Court to Mr. Nicholson.

> 'for that Ingenious and Serviceable performance'

together with an Explanation of the Table. Later in the same year it is noted

> 'Ordered (8th October) that a Message be sent to Mr. James Nicholson pewterer to his present Majesty King George to give him Notice to take up his ffreedom of this Company'.

In my view Mr. Nicholson more than earned his reward, but surely it is a little late in the day when pewter and pewtering was giving way to the march of time for such a table to be produced. The records indicate that in 1727-28

> 'It was ordered that a new assay mold be made as that in use was about *120 years old*'

These comments are made in no spirit of criticism, indeed had the writer been compiling the Nicholson Table, the Company would be well into the 21st century and beyond awaiting the result. The point at issue must be the question of the practical degree of accuracy available to the working pewterer weighing the metal content of his wares. One must submit that certainly in the 17th and 18th centuries and later, the attitude of many practical pewterers would have been the application of the 'rule of thumb', or 'near enough for country work' principle. Some examples especially of provincial pieces of 17th and 18th century manufacture support this v.ew. Taking the foregoing matters into account, we therefore return to Mr. Welch's 'History of the Worshipful Company of Pewterers' for some positive indication as to the system of weights being used in the early 17th century which can be reconciled to the avoirdupois weights recorded in the accompaniments to the photographs. In the 'Additional Appendix to the History of the Worshipful Company of Pewterers' Note 2 Page 3 will be found on the line commencing

Pcent = per cent 'and more relevantly to our case' In minerals = per Cwt. = 100lb. not 112lb.'

In the 'Candlesticks with Bawles' assay of 1612-13 is given the weight of a pair of candlesticks grawnd as 04 di lbs, which may be taken I think to be $4\frac{1}{2}$lbs ie. $2\frac{1}{4}$lbs for a single one. In our survey, the only ball-knopped candlestick which in any way approaches this weight is Ball Knop No. 1, the avoirdupois weight of which is, with the weight of the sconce included — 2lbs.

In the 1612-13 syzeing a single candlestick grawnd should weigh $2\frac{1}{4}$lbs, but our research (if that is not too pompous a word) points to Ball Knop No. 1 having been made in the late 1630s or early 1640s. The missing $\frac{1}{4}$lb may have been attributable to today's avoirdupois weight failing to correspond with those weights to which reference has been made in the 1612-1613 syzeing, or alternatively to the latter weights having diminished in practical terms as the century wore on. There are obviously other explanations associated with my earlier remarks suggesting that mathematical considerations probably occupied little of the working pewterer's day. A glance through 'The Weights and Measurers of England' by R. D. Connor indicates some of the complexities involved. To quote from Page 332 of Professor Connor's work —

'Although steps were being taken to endeavour to regulate and control British metrology it cannot be said that even by the mid-nineteenth century uniformity had been achieved. Indeed the Report of 1862 referred to earlier contains the following cri de coeur: 49

The silent influence of usage has baffled the decrees of legislation; and we are still far distant from the uniformity at which we have so often, yet so vainly aimed'.

Perhaps the matter may be summed up in an adaptation of a rather well used, but trenchant remark attributed to the former Trade Unionist — the late Mr. Vic Feather.

'Metrology, they talk of nothing else in Barnsley'.

In the absence therefore of someone coming up with a better effort the suggestion to readers is that Ball Knop No. 1 is and was always intended to be a CANDLESTICK WITH BAWLE GRAWND.

BALL KNOP No. 1

THE GREAT GRAND-PARENT

Height (overall with sconce fitted)	8½ inches
Weight of candlestick	1lb 11ozs
Weight of sconce	5ozs
Combined weight	2lbs (avoirdupois)
Interior diameter of candlestick nozzle	1⅕ inches (approx)
Exterior diameter of candlestick nozzle	1⅖ inches (approx)
Interior diameter of sconce nozzle	1$\frac{1}{10}$ inches (approx)
Overall diameter of sconce flange	3⅘ inches
Upper stem fillet (double impressed lines above and below)	1$\frac{7}{10}$ inches wide
Knop — plain ball	2⅘ inches wide (approx)
Base — circular — diameter	7⅕ inches

Base type — *flanged surround* rising to a mound protecting a recessed form of drip pan. Indications are that this is a feature of manufacture and not a convenience modification.

Ownership marks — M I B

Maker's hall marks — (three) these consist of three escutcheons, the first of which contains the barely visible letters 'R C' and the number '36', whilst the other two contain a six petalled flower perhaps a daisy. The craftsmanship of the dye maker in this instance in creating the blend of the punch marks appears quite ingenious.

––––––––

A number of years ago, the writer had the opportunity, sadly not taken up to buy this candlestick and whilst this piece, now is owned by someone else, it has a special place in the affections. It is believed to be perhaps the earliest surviving member of the pewter ball knop family made a little earlier than 1640. Its general appearance and gut feeling suggest the early nature of the piece, but fascinatingly the assiduous researches of Dr. Law provide some corroboration of the likely maker of the specimen. Mr. Gabriel Butcher, a member of the twelve 'Certain Tryffeleres' chosen for the assay of 1612-1613 where the 'Candlesticks with Bawles' are first mentioned, took unto himself an apprentice *Robert Crimpe* in 1625 until 1632. The said Robert set up shop in *1636* and paid quarterage from 1636 to 1642 and was deceased by 1644. The son of William Crimpe, Robert originated from Wrantwich in

Somerset and his apprentices were Edward Heath and Peter Duffield. Being apprenticed to a Tryffeler and hence a maker of amongst other things — candlesticks, we have Robert presenting himself for recognition as the maker of the Great Grandparent of all our known ball knops. At 2lbs avoirdupois weight (with sconce) compared with the $2\frac{1}{4}$ lbs weight shown on the 1612-1613 syzeing for bawle Candlesticks Grawnd — the heaviest weight on the syzeing, can Ball Knop 1, the heaviest-weighted encountered in this study, be other than a 1630 — ish Candlestick with bawle Grawnd?

BALL KNOP No. 2

GRANDPARENT ONE

Height	5½ inches
Weight	10½ ounces (avoirdupois)
Interior diameter of candlestick nozzle	1 inch (approx)
Overall diameter across flange	1⅚ inches
Upper stem fillet (double impressed lines above and below)	⅖ inches wide
Knop	— plain ball
Base	— circular — diameter 5¼ inches
Base type	— *flanged surround* — base of stem recessed into pedestal to form a drip pan — appears to be a feature of manufacture rather than convenience modification
Decoration	— faint sign of beaded decoration round pedestal
Marks	— none visible perhaps attributable to minor repair on flange

———

This candlestick together with its fellow *Grandparent Two* has certain similarities to *Great Grand-parent,* although there is no firm evidence that it or its fellow has ever had a separate sconce. Such similarities include a broad fillet with double impressed lines above and below; a plain ball; the base of the stem recessed by design into the pedestal to form a drip pan and the flange surrounding the whole of the circular base. The slight differences in weight and height between this piece and its companion Ball Knop No. 3 do not appear to be entirely attributable to the small repair to this stick, but the rather wider than normal nozzle diameter may be suggestive of the original presence of separate sconces although the width of the flange compared with that of Ball Knop 1 does not add support to this.

BALL KNOP No. 3

GRANDPARENT TWO

Height	5¾ inches
Weight	9½ ounces (avoirdupois)

Other dimensions and details as shown for Grandparent One ie Ball Knop 2 unless otherwise stated

Marks   Maker's touch on flange — apparently a fleur de lys and letters P S in a diamond.

Whilst this candlestick is the lifelong companion of Grandparent One, it will be noted that the weights and heights of the two are not identical, an irritating discrepancy with which technological twentieth century brains are unable to cope, but to the maker and no doubt the present owner such 'trifles' have never mattered.

See comments concerning Ball Knop No. 2.

BALL KNOP No. 4

GRANDPARENT THREE

Height		6½ inches
Weight		1lb 1 ounce (avoirdupois)
Interior diameter of candlestick nozzle		1$\frac{1}{10}$ inches (approx)
Overall diameter across flange		1$\frac{1}{5}$ inches (approx)
Upper stem	— plain — without fillet	
Knop	— damaged — see comments hereunder — diameter	2$\frac{3}{5}$ inches
Base	— octagonal — width	4$\frac{7}{10}$ inches
Maker's mark	— initials 'R B' with a small blip	

Perhaps the present possessors of this sad fellow will forgive the attention drawn to the ill treatment to which this mid 17th century candlestick has been subjected in antiquity. Many readers will recognise it from H. H. Cotterell's 'Old Pewter Its Makers and Marks' where it is depicted on page 90 item b. This piece seems to be the only survivor of the 17th century with an octagonal base of equal sides and referring back to a comment in the introduction to this book that this was a type mentioned by Randle Holme in 1649, one can perhaps agree with Cotterell that it is possibly of 'the late Commonwealth period'. Instinct suggests that this is a few years earlier and mention has been heard of the fact that an octagonal salt mould may have been used to form a base for this article. With this assertion the writer would disagree. Examination suggests that the base was formed from a candlestick mould per se for a reason connected with the underside of the base, which owing to lack of examples is at present inadequately researched and which must therefore be left unsaid. In addition it will be noted on Page 95 Vol. 2 of Welch's 'History of the Worshipful Company of Pewterers' 1635-36 on 23rd February, Richard March was censured 'for making peece basons out of the foote mould out of a Candlestick'. The inference seems to be that at this early period, at least in London, use of moulds for purposes of manufacturing items for which they were not intended was not viewed with any favour by the Company. Indeed it is unlikely that conformation to weight requirements could have been maintained had willy nilly use been made of the moulds. In the suggestion earlier relating to DATING OF THE BALL KNOP, it will be seen that the trumpet base of an 18th century paten made by E. Fairbrother is similar to later trumpet-based candlesticks. Without trying to justify the unjustifiable in this contradiction, the Fairbrother paten was made in the north west of

England almost a hundred years later than poor Richard March was censured and the question must be asked, would you obey the wishes of a by-now toothless bulldog in London in 1635-36, whilst trying to scrape a living in a fading way of life in another century? Whether you accept this or not, Grandparent Three is an early and historically important candlestick.

Now to the vandalizing of this specimen. Cotterell's portrayal of this piece merely shows a photograph of what appears to be a half ball knop with a slight swelling at the upper part of the stem. To our photographer James Johnson must go the credit for questioning from the photograph as to whether this candlestick may be a true but damaged ball knop. Such in fact seems the case. On examination it will be seen that some antiquarian ostrogoth has forced an iron sleeve into the mouth of the nozzle and the bulge visible in the picture marks the point at which the sleeve terminates. Not content with this someone, no doubt the same person has inserted an ill fitting iron push rod through the underside of the candlestick stem so as to emerge into the iron sleeve. The rim round the nozzle mouth is but $\frac{3}{10}$ inches wide and therefore cannot be classed as a candlestick flange in the true sense of the present context and my bet is that this candlestick has had a separate sconce which has in the passage of time been lost. With the advent of push rods, it would seem that some, for want of more appropriate but crueller words, 'amateur craftsman' has modified the stick to take a smaller diameter candle and contrived a push rod to eject or prolong the stump ends. The result of forcing the iron sleeve into the candlestick nozzle would appear to have depressed the stem into the top half of the seamed ball, which in turn has collapsed into the lower portion of the ball and in effect created a separate style which never caught on. Should this seem to be unnecessarily harsh on the person improvising the candlestick, poverty rather than parsimony may have been the motivation and sympathetic restoration could work wonders. Distortion and improvisation renders the nozzle dimension and weight devoid of significance.

The candlestick is in the collection of the Fitzwilliam Museum in Cambridge and for the record, although it scarcely needs to be said, the specimen's present condition is in no way attributable to any mis-treatment by its present owners, who undoubtedly exercise the utmost care in preserving all the items in their charge. Reference to the earlier mentioned photograph in Cotterell's work confirms the general condition of the candlestick and its distorted stem many years before it passed into the caring hands of the Fitzwilliam. One must sympathise with the point of view expressed by the Director of the Museum, Mr. Simon Jervis that the piece should not be altered from its present state for the reasons that (a) there is no certainty as to what it was originally like and (b) that the alterations are part of its structural history. However, if this work has any value, the illustrations of the various forms of the ball knop suggest something of the characteristics one might expect to find in the type, and museums, dealers and collectors alike can only benefit from the knowledge. The piece seems unique and it is to the advantage of all that we are fortunate to behold it and wonder.

Accession Number - 91 - 1933. Photograph reproduced by kind permission of the Syndics of the Fitzwilliam Museum Cambridge.

BALL KNOP No. 5

Height		6½ inches
Weight		10 ounces (avoirdupois)
Interior diameter of candlestick nozzle		¾ inches
Overall diameter of flange		1½ inches
Upper stem fillet	— two turned rings above and below unobtrusive worn fillet	
Knop	— plain round ball without fillet	
Base	— octangular — width	3¹⁵⁄₁₆ inches
Base type	— rising in a plinth from an octangular pedestal as	
	* manufactured	
Decoration	— none	
Marks	— no evidence of marks	

———

The plain unfilleted ball on this specimen suggests that the piece is one of the earlier octangular specimens.

---

* Distortions sometimes found in the ball knop type of candlestick, by either depressing the stem into the base to form a drip tray or more rarely pushing up the recessed drip tray to form a plinth perhaps require some mention of the writer's view of the form in which the appropriate pieces were originally manufactured.

BALL KNOP No. 6

Height		6½ inches
Weight		10 ounces (avoirdupois)
Interior diameter of candlestick nozzle		7⁄10 inches
Overall diameter of flange, which has been	depressed into an eave shape — probably a modification to provide extra light	1½ inches
Upper stem fillet	— incised circles above and below a quite prominent cast single fillet	
Knop	— plain round ball without fillet	
Base	— octangular — width	3⅘ inches
Base type	— rising in a plinth from an octangular pedestal as manufactured	
Decoration	— a pattern of milling is present above the octangular base	
Marks	— no evidence of a maker's touch, but in good lighting a scratched mark 16-56? is visible. On the inside of the base is a punched letter 'E' in an escutcheon on the right of which is an incused letter 'M'. The late Mr Richard Mundey attributed this mark to the piece having at some time been in the Mount Edgecumbe stable	

This candlestick is a very sturdy intact specimen and the flange having been depressed all round in earlier years only adds to the attraction. Perhaps I may be permitted to use the expression 'flangelized', in cases where the flange has been modified as the handiwork of some earlier possessor. The plain ball is again possibly indicative of this candlestick having been one of the earlier octangular-based pieces produced.

BALL KNOP No. 7

Height		6 inches
Weight		10½ ounces (avoirdupois)
Interior diameter of candlestick nozzle		⅘ inches
Flange	— flange has been restored, perhaps unfortunately and inappropriately with a square type, with rounded corners — width	1½ inches
Upper stem fillet	— quite pronounced cast single fillet	
Knop	— round plain ball without fillet	
Base	— octangular — width	3⁹⁄₁₀ inches
Base type	— rising in a plinth from an octangular pedestal as manufactured	
Decoration	— a pattern of milling is present above octangular base	
Marks	— no evidence of a maker's touch or ownership marks	

———

Several similar characteristics can be noted between this specimen and ball-knop No. 6 and I personally, have no doubt that it originally had a circular flange and may even have had the same maker. Oh for a touch mark!

Accession Number 89 - 1933 Photograph reproduced by kind permission of the syndics of the Fitzwilliam Museum Cambridge.

BALL KNOP No. 8

Height		6½ inches
Weight		9¼ ounces (avoirdupois)
Interior diameter of candlestick nozzle		9⁄10 inches
Overall diameter of flange		1½ inches
Upper stem fillet	— fairly wide and consisting of three impressed lines to portray a double fillet	
Knop	— plain round ball with fillet	
Base	— circular — diameter almost	4 inches
Base type	— recessed form of drip pan protected by a circular mound. There appears to be some evidence that the base was made in this form, but indications of physical pressure having been applied to further depress plinth into base	
Decoration	— faint circular lines round base mound	
Marks	— ownership mark which may be 'A C' and possible trace of touch	

This fascinating piece has an early feel, given substance by the wider than customary fillet appearance. It has some unsightly scale, removal of which could perhaps only prove advantageous in improving both the conservation and display of the specimen.

Accession Number M 144 - 1930 By courtesy of the Trustees of the Victoria and Albert Museum.

BALL KNOP No. 9

Height	6⁵⁄₁₆ inches
Weight	9 ounces (avoirdupois)
Interior diameter of candlestick nozzle	$\frac{4}{5}$ inches
Overall diameter of flange	— circular —
	— a trace of old repair
Upper stem fillet	— none
Knop	— fairly flattish plain ball with slightly raised fillet
Base	— circular — diameter 4 inches
Base type	— recessed form of drip pan protected by circular mound as manufactured
Decoration	— circular line round base mound
Marks	— trace of ownership initials on top of flange. No touch visible, but this could have been obliterated by old minor repair to flange

---

This ball-knop is understood to have originally surfaced in Wales and because of its similarity to ball knop No. 10, which also appeared at a Cardiff auction, may have been made in or around the Bristol area — see comments on ball knop No. 10.

BALL KNOP No. 10

Height	6½ inches
Weight	10 ounces (avoirdupois)
Interior diameter of candlestick nozzle	$\frac{9}{10}$ inches
Overall diameter of flange — circular —	$1\frac{15}{16}$ inches
Upper stem fillet	— pronounced fillet $\frac{1}{5}$ of inch wide with a pair of incised circles above and a pair below
Knop	— plain ball with pronounced fillet
Base	— circular — diameter 4½ inches
Base type	— recessed form of drip pan protected by circular mound as manufactured
Decoration	— two circular lines round base mound
Marks	— *at long last* — a maker's mark 'E G' and a separate letter 'B' on flange attributed to Edward Gregory of Bristol: see H. H. Cotterell's 'Old Pewter — Its Makers and Marks' No. 2001: mentioned in 1694 with his wife Anne. He was dead in 1695. Flange also bears ownership marks initials 'G H'

Together with a plate of 13 inches diameter and a small dome lid tankard, both bearing the maker's mark of Richard Going of Bristol this specimen was purchased at a Cardiff auction in 1991. After cleaning and restoration by an old maestro, all were found to bear the 'G H' ownership marks, the mark on the candlestick being larger and of different form and therefore unlikely to have been punched at the same time as the other two. These items were part of a lot of five. All were well oxidised and dusty and did not seem to have been in the public domain for many years. A particularly special find indeed. By the way, who was 'G H'?

BALL KNOP No. 11

Height		6⅝ inches
Weight		9½ ounces (avoirdupois)
Interior diameter of candlestick nozzle		⅞ inches
Overall diameter across flange		1⅝ inches
Upper stem fillet	— twin hoop bands in relief	
Knop	— divided by narrow band in relief	
Base	— circular — diameter	4 inches
Base type	— recessed to form drip pan — probably as manufactured —	
Decoration	— has integral flange round base	
Marks	— None discernible	

———

Of this piece, the late Richard Mundey has written — 'An identical specimen is illustrated in H. H. Cottrell's 'Old Pewter — Its Makers & Marks' on Plate XXII, fig. a. that was in the Port Collection. English c. 1680. (Unmarked): Amongst photographs from Richard's collection, now in the possession of the Pewter Society is depicted what is probably the same candlestick, here illustrated in perhaps a rather less loved condition than was acceptable to its present owner.

BALL KNOP No. 12

Height	7⅛ inches
Weight	9⅗ ounces (avoirdupois)
Internal diameter of candlestick nozzle	¹⁵⁄₁₆ inches
Overall diameter of flange	1¾ inches
Upper stem fillet — circular indentations to form triple fillets	
Knop — plain ball encircled by rather unobtrusive fillet	
Base — circular trumpet style — diameter	4⅛ inches
Base type — rising in a plinth from circular pedestal surrounded by incised circular line to pedestal base surrounded by an outward-sloping flange	
Decoration — none	
Marks — no evidence of ownership or maker's marks	

————

Yet another style illustrating the individualistic traits of its maker. By comparison with others of its ilk, its triple fillets and absence of recess below the plinth make an interesting distinction. Not the type for 'milady's boudoir' perhaps, but a loveable 'journeyman'.

By kind permission of the Colonial Williamsburg Foundation — Accession No. 1960 - 316. Photograph (c) Delmore A Wenzel Formerly in the Sutherland Graham Collection.

BALL KNOP No. 13

THE WEE LAD

Height	$3\frac{4}{5}$ inches
Weight	7 ounces (avoirdupois)
Interior diameter of candlestick nozzle	$\frac{7}{10}$ inches
Overall diameter of flange	$1\frac{1}{2}$ inches
Upper stem fillet — two faint rings round stem	$\frac{1}{12}$ of an inch apart
Knop — plain but with fillet	
Base — circular — diameter	3 inches
Base type — slightly recessed round base of stem — undoubtedly a feature of manufacture	
Decoration — two turned rings about $\frac{1}{12}$ of an inch apart just above base of stem	
Marks — possible trace of unidentifiable mark on flange	

To the candlestick enthusiast is this not the most charming of all ball-knopped candlesticks? The diameter of the nozzle, which corresponds in size to some of the others depicted is indicative of the fact that this piece has always been intended to be a candlestick and not a taperstick. A repair has been carried out in antiquity to about $1\frac{1}{2}$ inch section of the trumpet type base and to stabilise this repair, a pewter base has been applied. Even the repair seems enchanting, but it does mean that the stick would be perhaps two ounces lighter without it than the 7 ounces shown above.

BALL KNOP No. 14

Height		7½ inches
Weight		11 ounces (avoirdupois)
Interior diameter of candlestick nozzle		1 inch
Overall diameter of flange		2 inches
Upper stem fillet	— worn single fillet	
Knop	— plain with bold fillet	
Base	— circular trumpet type — diameter	4¹⁄₁₂ inches
Base type	— circular trumpet style with ridged pedestal, which is surrounded by narrow flange	
Decoration	— nothing other than ridge and flange as outlined in base type	
Marks	— none discernible	

———

This style seems to fit in at the later end of the dating spectrum and whilst one which the writer has seen probably dates to about 1675, judging from form and condition, this specimen is perhaps just pre-1700. The c.1675 piece was formerly in the Minchin collection. It was a great favourite with John and as its whereabouts are now uncertain, it has not been possible to include it in this survey. However it has been illustrated several times in several publications, including the Society's Journal of Autumn 1981.

BALL KNOP No. 15

Height		6⅜ inches
Weight		9 ounces (avoirdupois)
Interior diameter of candlestick nozzle		$1\frac{1}{16}$ inches
Flange	— this has been depressed into a rolled over form — therefore overall measurement	$1\frac{5}{16}$ inches
Upper stem fillet	— pronounced single fillet	
Knop	— plain but with fillet	
Base	— octangular — width	$3\frac{15}{16}$ inches
Base type	— rising in plinth from an octangular pedestal as manufactured	
Decoration	— gadrooning at base of stem where it meets the pedestal	
Marks	— no evidence of ownership or maker's marks	

————

An attractive little candlestick, which like those following are highly prized by those fortunate enough to own one . . . or more.

BALL KNOP No. 16

Height	almost 6½ inches
Weight	9¼ ounces (avoirdupois)
Interior diameter of nozzle	$\frac{9}{10}$ inches
Overall flange diameter	1½ inches
Upper stem fillet	— worn and less conspicuous than the preceding specimen — ball knop No. 15
Knop	— plain but with fillet
Base	— octangular — width 4 inches
Base type	— rising in plinth from an octangular pedestal — as manufactured
Decoration	— gadrooning at base of stem where it meets the octangular pedestal
Marks	— no evidence of ownership or maker's marks

Similar in form to ball knop No. 15, but the flange remains unbowed by time and tinkerers.

BALL KNOP No. 17

Height	5⅘ inches
Weight	9 ounces (avoirdupois)
Interior diameter of candlestick nozzle	$\frac{7}{10}$ inches
Overall diameter of flange	$1\frac{7}{10}$ inches
Upper stem fillet	— single worn and not over-emphasised fillet
Knop	— evidence of worn gadrooning on upper and lower halves of the knop, which has fillet
Base	— octangular — width $3\frac{7}{10}$ inches
Base type	— rising in a plinth from an octangular pedestal as manufactured
Marks	— worn gadrooning above the octangular base There are traces of a possible touch mark on the flange, but to my eyes this is not distinguishable

———

This charmer is once again being hawked through public pages having previously appeared in 'The Connoisseur' some 35 years ago and in other publications. It has been described as having had 'A tiny touch upon the lip with the initials 'T B' in a diamond' and was I understand previously in the R. W. Cooper collection. Apologies for once again ignominiously frog-marching it through the present hit parade but a thing of beauty is a joy for ever. If the initials of the maker are on this piece and are or were 'T B', researches turned up about thirty odd possible pewterers who may have produced this candlestick — and even so it could have been someone else.

BALL KNOP No. 18

Height		$6\frac{3}{8}$ inches
Weight		$8\frac{19}{20}$ ounces (avoirdupois)
Interior diameter of candlestick nozzle		$\frac{3}{4}$ inches
Overall diameter of flange	— convex shaped and encircled with incised line	$1\frac{1}{2}$ inches
Upper stem fillet	— impressed on either side of fairly prominent fillet	
Knop	— gadrooned ball encircled by bold fillet	
Base	— octangular - width	$3\frac{13}{16}$ inches
Base type	— rising in a plinth from an octangular pedestal — as manufactured	
Decoration	— gadrooned at base of stem above the junction with the octangular pedestal	
Marks	— No evidence of ownership or maker's marks	

Whilst the opportunity of viewing this pleasant looking candlestick at first hand, has not presented itself, it would seem that from the consistent regularity of the convex flange, this variation is a feature of its manufacture and one of the few examples where this appears to be the case. This piece was formerly in the possession of A. H. Isher & Son Cheltenham.

By kind permission of the Colonial Willinamsburg Foundation — Accession Number - 1958 - 597. (c) Photograph Delmore A. Wenzel.

BALL KNOP No. 19

Height		6 inches
Weight		9½ ounces (avoirdupois)
Interior diameter of candlestick nozzle		$\frac{7}{10}$ to $\frac{8}{10}$ inches
	— difficult to measure accurately owing to flange distortion	
Flange	— this has been distorted into a rolled over form — therefore no measurement	
Upper stem fillet	— pronounced single fillet	
Knop	— plain but with fillet	
Base	— octangular — width —	$3^{15}\!/_{16}$ inches
Base type	— octangular pedestal into which base of stem is recessed to a depth of perhaps half an inch. The owner's view is that this is in part as a consequence of manufacture and in part of distortion. This delightful little candlestick is quite similar in appearance to ball knop No. 15 which is slightly taller and the absence of the recession in the base may compensate for this minor difference in height.	
Decoration	— worn gadrooning at base of stem where it meets with the pedestal	
Marks	— no evidence of ownership or maker's marks	

Like its fellow ball knops of this general style, this type is perhaps the most favoured by all collectors.

BALL KNOP No. 20

Height	6½ inches
Weight	8¾ ounces (avoirdupois)
Interior diameter of candlestick nozzle	9/10 inches
Overall diameter of flange — circular with protecting flange	1⅗ inches
Upper stem fillet	— quite pronounced form
Knop	— gadrooned above and below a pronounced fillet
Base	— octangular width 3 9/10 inches
Base type	— plinth recessed into form of drip pan and surrounded by circular mound — on octangular pedestal — as manufactured
Decoration	— in addition to above gadrooned knop, the protecting mound round the drip pan area is also decorated with gadrooning
Mark	— trace of maker's mark (beyond recognition) on flange

This is one of a fine pair of highly collectable sticks, there being a slight variation in weight between this and its fellow - ball knop No. 21.

BALL KNOP No. 21

Height	6½ inches
Weight	8½ ounces (avoirdupois)

Upper stem fillet fairly pronounced but slightly eroded.
Other dimensions and details as shown for ball-knop No. 18 unless otherwise stated

Mark	— no trace of any visible mark

Whilst the ball-knop candlestick is a rare bird, a pair of such sticks is almost like two people having the same sets of fingerprints.

BALL KNOP No. 22

Height		$6\frac{1}{2}$	inches
Weight		$10\frac{3}{4}$	ounces (avoirdupois)
Interior diameter of candlestick nozzle		$\frac{9}{10}$	inches
Overall diameter of flange		$1\frac{1}{2}$	inches
Upper stem fillet	— has a prominent single fillet, which appears part of the stem casting		
Knop	— gadrooning above and below the filleted knop		
Base	— octangular — width	$4\frac{1}{5}$	inches
Base type	— plinth is recessed into base to form a drip pan surrounded by protecting mound above octangular pedestal — as manufactured		
Decoration	— in addition to the above gadrooning of the knop, the protecting mound of the base is also gadrooned. Further knurling in miniature at the junction of the top of the stem and underside of the flange is an unusual embellishment		
Marks	— a maker's touch consisting of a diamond shaped lozenge containing what may be a fleur de lys		

This fine candlestick has appeared in several publications and its quality perhaps suggests it to be the work of a London maker.

Accession Number M77 - 1945 By courtesy of the Trustees of the Victoria and Albert Museum.

BALL KNOP No. 23

Height		6 inches
Weight		10¼ ounces (avoirdupois)
Interior diameter of candlestick nozzle almost		1 inch
Flange	— has a rolled over distortion not as part of manufacture — therefore not measured	
Upper stem fillet	— bold fillet with seam above and below	
Knop	— emphatic gadrooning above and below pronounced fillet	
Base	— octangular — width	4½ inches
Base type	— plinth of stem base recessed to form a drip pan and surrounded by a circular gadrooned mound above the octangular pedestal — as manufactured	
Decoration	— fine gadrooning as above on knop and base mound	
Marks	— Maker's touch in the shape of the lower part of a heart on the flange, near some of those frustrating marks upon which the reader may like to make his own judgement from the photographs of Ball Knop Nos. 23 and 24	

This candlestick together with ball knop No. 24 is again one of a very rare pair and a minor variation in weight also exists between the two.

BALL KNOP No. 24

Height   6 inches
Weight   10 ounces (avoirdupois)
Other dimensions and details as shown for ball knop No. 23 unless otherwise stated

Marks   — maker's touch in the outline of a heart visible.
                         Please note also the other flange mark which depends on which way one holds the candlestick or photograph of same as to the view obtained

A heart appears in a number of maker's touches recorded. Without further detail no identification is possible, but in any event no similar mark appears to have been recorded.

BALL KNOP No. 25

Height	7¼ inches
Weight	13⅗ ounces (avoirdupois)
Internal diameter of candlestick nozzle	$^{15}\!/_{16}$ inches
Overall diameter of flange — roll top type	1¾ inches
Upper stem fillet	— modest, cast single fillet
Knop	— plain ball encircled by unobtrusive fillet
Base	— circular — diameter 4$^{15}\!/_{16}$ inches
Base type	— the base of the stem is recessed into the round pedestal and as the photograph well illustrates was no doubt cast in this form originally
Decoration	— emphatic gadrooning on the base surround
Marks	— no evidence of ownership or maker's marks

Compared with others of its style, this is a weightier specimen and of robust construction. Its flange has a rather unevenly rolled over shape consistent with it having been 'flangelized'. Could this be one of John Shorey's 'mid' or 'large knurled' creations? See details of Ball Knop No. 27. This piece is also a former specimen of the A. H. Isher and Son Cheltenham stable.

By kind permission of the Colonial Williamsburg Foundation
Accession Number — 1966 - 297 (c) Photograph Delmore A. Wenzel

BALL KNOP No. 26

Height	5½ inches
Weight	10¾ ounces (avoirdupois)
Interior diameter of candlestick nozzle	⁹⁄₁₀ inches
Overall diameter of flange — flange has been apparently subject to some restoration and this measurement has no original significance	2 inches (almost)
Upper stem fillet — bold single fillet	
Knop — gadrooned on either side of a wide fillet	
Base — circular — diameter	4 inches
Base type — the base of the stem is recessed into the round pedestal to form a drip pan and was probably made originally in this form	
Decoration — gadrooned ball as outlined above and also gadrooning on the base surround	

The impression is that this candlestick was formerly in the collection of the later Mr. Christopher Peal as depicted on page 104 of his 'British Pewter'. An interesting comparison may be drawn between this piece and the specimen shown later as ball knop No. 30 in relation to the base type. What is your opinion?

BALL KNOP No. 27

Height		6½ inches
Weight		12 ounces (avoirdupois)
Interior diameter of candlestick nozzle		1³⁄₁₆ inches
Overall diameter of flange		1¾ inches
Upper stem fillet	— bold fillet with seam above and below	
Knop	— emphatic gadrooning above and below a pronounced fillet	
Base	— circular — diameter	4⁷⁄₁₀ inches
Base type	— stem base recessed to form a drip pan as manufactured	
Decoration	— in addition to above gadrooning of knop, further positive gadrooning surrounds the base wall	
Marks	— the top part of a diamond shaped touch containing the tops of letters which appear to be I S below small inverted 'V' shaped object, like a leaf with three points	

———

This is a finely wrought candlestick in remarkable condition and probably the work of a London maker. The I S touch, if such it is could have belonged to one of a number of makers of the late 17th or earlier part of the 18th century. As Colonel John Shorey was apparently a maker of flatware in addition to which there is no evidence of his use of a diamond shaped touch, he is an unlikely candidate to have made this candlestick. However, we are indebted to Dr. R. F. Homer for the information that in a 1716 inventory of the Shorey stock, 300 candlesticks in eight different patterns are recorded. To quote from Dr. Homer's letter — these include —

26 pairs large knurled
12 pairs mid ditto
12 pairs small ditto
14 pairs large diamond
29 pairs small ditto
12 pairs mid H B candlesticks   weight 18 lbs
20 pairs small ditto
 5 water candlesticks

Questions may be asked here —

Is this fine candlestick a candlestick knurled?

A personal view is that H B may stand for 'High Bell' referring to the well known high bell based candlestick, which have been thought to belong to a period more than 100 years earlier. The belief is that the weights of some are more consistent with a later rather than earlier date. Perhaps this speculation may lead to more light being shed on the topic. It is unpalatable for anyone to think that a prized piece is later than one assumed, but any candlesticks of the types under discussion are highly desirable. There will never be any more of the genuine ones in existence than there are now and a closed mind will never learn the truth. Does the mention of a knurled candlestick provide another hint of the manufacture of ball knops in the 18th century?

A present day pewter manufacturer has indicated that he understood the word 'knurled' to refer to the 'chattering' effect of tooling decoration and in present day terminology it may well do so. However, Chambers Twentieth Century Dictionary defines the word knurl as follows: —

'Knurl, nurl, a small excrescence or protuberance: a ridge of bead, esp. in series, as in the milling of a screw head; 'and goes on to say' — adj. knurled (spelt gnarled, Shak., Measure for Measure, folio 1623) covered with knurls. n. knurling, *mouldings* or other woodwork elaborated into *a series of knobs!* It has been suggested in a number of works on pewter that pewter candlesticks went out of fashion for much of the eighteenth century, so one last question concerning this matter — how come John Shorey had 300 candlesticks in stock in 1716? *Accession Number CS 14* By kind permission of the National Trust Arlington Court.

BALL KNOP No. 28

Height		7½ inches
Weight		12¼ ounces (avoirdupois)
Interior diameter of candlestick nozzle		⅞ inches
Overall diameter of flange		1¾ inches
Upper stem fillet	— emphatic cast fillet, flanged both above and below	
Knop	— gadrooned ball above and below a positive fillet	
Base	— octangular — width	4⁵⁄₁₆ inches
Base type	— rising in a plinth from an octangular pedestal as manufactured	
Decoration	— gadrooned at junction of base of stem above junction with octangular pedestal	
Marks	— no evidence of ownership or maker's marks	

One of a pair, its fellow being ball knop No. 29, these fine candlesticks are not identical with other gadrooned pairs illustrated in this book, in that the bases are unrecessed. Apart from other minor differences, they weigh rather heavier, doubtless placing them in another assay category.

By kind permission of the Colonial Williamsburg Foundation — Accession Number — 1961 — 215 Photograph Delmore A. Wenzle (c). It is understood the pair came into the possession of the Foundation from a Mr. and Mrs. Jacobs in Massachusetts.

BALL KNOP No. 29

Height	7½ inches
Weight	12⁷⁄₂₀ ounces (avoirdupois)

Unless otherwise stated details as shown for its partner Ball Knop No. 28

As will be noted from the photograph, the two candlesticks have some slight variations, the one in the background having apparently had some restoration round the base of the plinth. This may account for the minor difference in weight between the two.

By kind permission of the Colonial Williamsburg Foundation — Accession Number — 1961 — 215. Photograph (c) Delmore A. Wenzel.

BALL KNOP No. 30

Height		6½ inches
Weight		almost 10 ounces (avoirdupois)
Interior diameter of candlestick nozzle		⅘ inches
Flange	— this is missing	
Upper stem fillet	— comprised of a broad rather unobtrusive band	
Knop	— gadrooning on either side of a broad fillet or banding	
Base	— circular — diameter	4 9/16 inches
Base type	— convex style rising to a plinth	
Decoration	— gadrooning on knop as stated above and gadrooning round the pedestal of the circular base	
Marks	— the missing flange has deprived us of any opportunity of tracing a maker for this piece. There are no ownership marks, but referring back to — *The Structure of the Ball Knop* — in this book under the heading of 3) *The Nozzle plate* — will be seen a mention of a seven point asterisk type mark *cast* into the nozzle base plate disc, which is in fact set into this candlestick and visible from its underside. Was it a cancellation mark from another piece or was it an aid to the pewterer to obtain a disc of metal of the correct measurement? Or neither?	

This candlestick can be seen in a photograph at the front of National Types of Old Pewter, when it appeared complete with flange in a Glasgow exhibition of 1924. The surgery used to remove the flange has not been particularly well executed. A candlestick 'knurled' might well be applied to this type also, the word perhaps being more appropriate than the term 'gadrooning'. *Accession Number C 1947* By kind permission of the Hunterian Museum and Art Gallery.

BALL KNOP No. 31

Height		$6\frac{7}{10}$ inches
Weight		$8\frac{3}{4}$ ounces (avoirdupois)
Interior diameter of candlestick nozzle		$\frac{9}{10}$ inches
Overall flange	— diameter	$1\frac{4}{5}$ inches
Upper stem fillet	— lacking prominence and consisting of two indented circles	
Knop	— plain with bold fillet	
Base	— circular trumpet type — diameter	$3\frac{4}{5}$ inches
Base type	— slightly convex and rising to a plinth, whilst the hint of a flange surrounds the base.	
Decoration	— If such it can be called consists of two circular lines at top of base pedestal	
Marks	— Maker's touch mark of shield shape containing a lion? and ownership mark 'A I' both situated on flange	

In sound condition, this candlestick like several to follow, has the general outline of a seventeenth century specimen, but the characteristics, including lack of wear and the superficial upper stem fillet, together with some almost indefinable sophistication lacking in earlier pieces, leads to an impression that it must date to no earlier than the first quarter of the eighteenth century. This suggestion does not in any way detract from the desirability of owning such a piece.

Accession Number M75 — 1938 By courtesy of the Trustees of the Victoria and Albert Museum.

BALL KNOP No. 32

Height		6⁹⁄₁₀ inches
Weight		9½ ounces (avoirdupois)
Interior diameter of candlestick nozzle — about		¾ inch
Overall flange	— diameter — almost	2 inches
Upper stem fillet	— two indented circles forming fillet which is not prominent	
Knop	— plain but with bold fillet	
Base	— circular trumpet type — diameter	4 inches
Base type	— slightly convex and rising to a plinth	
Decoration	— three circular rings between top of circular pedestal base and base of stem	
Marks	— maker's touch consisting of a square containing indistinct detail	

For these details acknowledgements to Mr. Hepburn Myrtle. It is understood that some slight tear damage exists at the base of the stem.

By courtesy of the Art Gallery of New South Wales. Accession Number M12. 1949

BALL KNOP No. 33

Height		6 inches
Weight		9 ounces (avoirdupois)
Interior diameter of candlestick		7⁄₁₀ inches
Overall flange	— diameter —	1⁷⁄₁₀ inches
Upper stem fillet	— none	
Knop	— plain with bold fillet	
Base	— circular trumpet type — diameter	3⅘ inches
Base type	— rather high base pedestal rising to a plinth	
Decoration	— ridging round base and top of pedestal base	
Marks	— no maker's or ownership marks	

This candlestick has also a later appearance and it will be noted that the upper stem fillet has been dispensed with entirely by its maker. It has been designed more for utility than exhibition by 20th century collectors.

BALL KNOP No. 34

Height		7½ inches
Weight		13½ ounces (avoirdupois)
Interior diameter of nozzle		almost 1 inch
Flange	— slightly sloping as manufactured — overall diameter —	1⁹⁄₁₀ inches
Upper stem fillet	— indented, modest fillet	
Knop	— plain with bold fillet	
Base	— circular trumpet type — diameter —	4⅝ inches
Base type	— circular trumpet type gently curved to meet the plinth of the stem base	
Decoration	— slight ridging at top of base pedestal	
Marks	— absolutely none	

———

This specimen is in fine condition and when first displayed at a Pewter Society vetting session, it was noted that several members dated it to about 1720, this at a time when all ball-knop candlesticks were believed by general consensus to date to the later seventeenth century. The interesting feature which presents itself here is the manufactured sloping flange, suggesting that some pewterers were at last beginning to appreciate some need for this improvement. It will be noted however, that our Great Grandfather Ball-Knop has the same feature on its detachable sconce. Just imagine all the bending and rolling down of flanges which could have been avoided if everyone had adopted this slight modification. A personal view is that this specimen is one of the last of the ball knops made in perhaps 1725.

BALL KNOP No. 35

Height		7 inches
Weight		$9\frac{9}{10}$ ounces (avoirdupois)
Interior diameter of candlestick nozzle		$\frac{7}{8}$ inches
Overall diameter of flange		$1\frac{31}{32}$ inches
Upper stem fillet	— positive moulding of single fillet	
Knop	— the top segment only of an undecorated ball	
Base	— circular trumpet style	
	— diameter	$4\frac{5}{8}$ inches
Base type	— rising in a plinth from a circular pedestal which is encircled by two platform mouldings and the pedestal itself stands on a further platform moulding	
Decoration	— circular inscribed line round top of flange visible	
Marks	— no evidence of ownership or maker's marks	

A pair which came into the possession of the Colonial Williamsburg Foundation via the Ishers of Cheltenham and therefore likely to be English. There seems no valid reason to leave them out of this publication merely because they are half ball knops. Were they a transitional style or a one-off? Were they a Friday night or Monday morning job? Was the metal running low? In the absence of evidence we can perhaps only take them as we find them. They are probably provincial and made a few years one way or the other on either side of 1700. It seems a good idea to put them near the end of the book, in order to maintain the photographic pattern.

By kind permission of the Colonial Williamsburg Foundation — Accession No. 1960 — 794 (c) Photograph Delmore A. Wenzel

BALL KNOP No. 36

Height	7 inches
Weight	9⅘ ounces (avoirdupois)

Unless otherwise stated details as shown for its fellow Ball Knop No. 35.

————

There is a minimal weight variation between this ball knop and its fellow traveller, a condition which does not appear to be attributable to any other reason than that the specimens were not mass — produced and what better reason is there for collecting anything?

By kind permission of the Colonial Williamsburg Foundation Accession Number — 1960 794 (c) Photograph Delmore A Wenzel

BALL KNOP No. 37

THE MAVERICK

Height	about 7½ inches	
Weight	13 ounces (avoirdupois)	
Interior diameter of nozzle	1⅕ inches	
Flange	— this is a narrow affair about ⅕ of an inch wide	
Upper stem fillet	— none	
Knop	— plain flattened ball with wide collars above and below	
Base	— circular trumpet shape — diameter	6⅖ inches
Base type	— slopes gently from a ridged pedestal to a plinth	
Decoration	— faint 'chattered' decoration just above top of pedestal	
Marks	— faint trace of maker's touch on top of flange and ownership initials 'A R' on underside of base	

———

In every family and society there is at least one non-conformist. The almost sophisticated collars above and below the knop are at variance with some other aspects of this stick. It was purchased in Yorkshire in 1991 and had an insulting ill-fitting sconce inserted in the nozzle opening. This has been removed. The piece has some age and must at least carry an eighteenth century dating, borne out by the punched ownership marks, which are consistent with the letters one sees on late 17th/early eighteenth century baluster measures. There seems no doubt that it was made with a detachable sconce, although it has a nozzle base plate inside the stem. A minor old repair is visible on the underside of the base. With the addition of the detachable sconce this piece no doubt should have had, its weight would have been about equivalent to a category in the Candlesticks with bawles syzeing of the 17th century, although which category one can only hazard a guess.

BALL KNOP No. 38

Height	about	6¾₁₀ inches
Interior diameter of candlestick nozzle		9⁄10 inches
Flange	— almost vestigial — diameter	1½ inches
Upper stem fillets	— a series of three ridged fillets	
Knop	— plain with very flattened ball	
Base	— circular trumpet type base — diameter	4½ inches
Base type	— circular pedestal recessed slightly downwards to base of stem	
Decoration	— ridged pedestal, slightly flanged	
Marks	— maker's touch on flange — heart shaped outline containing letters 'R' and 'B'	

By comparison with the preponderance of examples shown in this publication, one has some unease about accepting this specimen as an example of the family of British Ball Knops. Its general appearance does not suggest it to be British or particularly early, but perhaps some reader either at home or abroad may recognise the touch on the flange.

Accession Number M79 — 1945 By courtesy of the Trustees of the Victoria and Albert Museum.

BALL KNOP No. 39

Height		5⅘ inches
Weight		8 ounces (avoirdupois)
Interior diameter of candlestick nozzle — about		½ inch
Flange	— slightly convex — overall diameter	1⅖ inches
Upper stem fillets	— imitation fillet made by encircling the stem with two rings of small tool marks	
Knop	— plain with positive fillet	
Base	— circular trumpet shaped — diameter	3⁹⁄₁₀ inches
Base type	— sloping upwards from ridged circular pedestal to plinth forming stem base	
Decoration	— above the base pedestal is a series of small tool marks encircling the bottom of the plinth	
Marks	— no maker's or ownership marks. Looking up into the underside of the candlestick a small round circle can be seen inscribed on the underside of the nozzle base plate	

———

This piece appears to be a worthy twentieth century production of a ball knop candlestick. It would be difficult to confuse it with the real thing. Age and wear are, as the auctioneers say — wanting.

Accession Number 1976 — 33 By kind permission of the Authorities of the Cheltenham Art Gallery and Museums.

BALL KNOPS Nos. 40 and 41

Photographs of these two ball knops have been forwarded by courtesy of a private collector in the United States of America, through the kind offices of Mr. Peter Hornsby. The comparisons with these and those specimens depicted earlier in this book, which the writer would identify as British Ball Knops should be extremely helpful to readers.

BALL KNOP No. 40

Is referred to on the back of the photograph as one of a pair.

Height	10 inches
Base diameter	6¾ inches

Mark *inside base* — A device with the appearance of the head of a thistle with an interior design.

Writing inside base — RK/-/- c. 1710

On the back of the photograph also, the candlestick is referred to as 'English 1685'! Such experience as research has provided compels one to disagree with these sentiments. Nevertheless a candlestick is a candlestick etc . . .

BALL KNOP No. 41

Is described on the back of the photograph as hereunder.

Height	7½ inches
Base diameter	5½ inches
Flange (?)	3 inches

Marks on Flange (?) E. I.

There seems to be no reason to quarrel with the assertion that this candlestick is attributed to the Netherlands — c. 1700

———

Sincere appreciation to our American friend for this contribution.

CONTINENTAL BALL KNOPS

In the following publications photographs of Continental Ball Knops can be found : —

'Keur van tin' B DUBBE Page 235 No. 200

'Zinneiesserhandwerk und Zingerattin Oldenburg Ostfriesland und Osnabruck' T KOHLMANN Page 171

'Materialalien zur Volkskultur' A SCHMIDT Page 126 Nos 219-220

SHORT BIBLIOGRAPHY

Professor R. D. Connor — The Weights and Measures of England
HMSO 1987

H. H. Cotterell — Old Pewter Its Makers and Marks
B. T. Batsford Ltd. 1929

W. J. Cripps — Old English Plate
John Murray 1903

A. O. Curle — Domestic Candlesticks from the Fourteenth to the end of the Eighteenth Century
Proceedings of the Society of Antiquaries of Scotland
Neill and Company 1927

A. L. Hayward Editor — Lives of the Most Remarkable Criminals (Collected from Original Papers and Authentic Memoirs and published in 1735)
George Routledge and Sons Ltd. 1927

C. A. Peal — British Pewter
John Gifford 1971

R. J. A. Shelley — Wigan and Liverpool Pewterers
Transactions of the Historic Society of Lancashire and Cheshire 1946

A. V. Sutherland Graeme — Seventeenth Century Pewter Candlesticks
The Connoisseur April 1956

C. Welch — History of the Worshipful Company of Pewterers of the City of London
Blades East and Blades 1902

C. Welch — Additional Appendix to the History of the Pewterers Company
Headley Bros.
Journal of the Pewter Society
Autumn 1981 — Spring and Autumn 1982

Ball Knop No. 1

Ball Knop No. 1
Showing sconce detached from candlestick.

Ball Knop No. 1
Showing candlestick minus sconce.

Ball Knop No. 1
Showing sconce minus candlestick.

Ball Knop No. 2

Ball Knop No. 3

Ball Knop No. 3
Showing touch on flange.

Ball Knop No. 4
Owner: *Fitzwilliam Museum, Cambridge. Accession No. 91 - 1933.*

Ball Knop No. 4
Showing iron sleeve inserted into candlestick nozzle.
Owner: *Fitzwilliam Museum, Cambridge. Accession No. 91 - 1933.*

Ball Knop No. 4
Showing iron push rod inserted into candlestick base.
Owner: *Fitzwilliam Museum, Cambridge. Accession No. 91 - 1933.*

Ball Knop No. 5

Ball Knop No. 6

Ball Knop No. 7
Owner: *Fitzwilliam Museum, Cambridge. Accession No. 89 - 1933.*

Ball Knop No. 8
Owner: *Victoria and Albert Museum, London. Accession No. M144 - 1930.*

Ball Knop No. 9

Ball Knop No. 10

Plate 10(a)
Plate, Dome lid tankard and Ball Knop candlestick.

Plate 10(b)
Initials 'G.H.' on Candlestick, Dome lid Tankard and Plate.

Ball Knop No. 11

Ball Knop No. 11(a) — (see Ball Knop No. 11).

Ball Knop No. 12
Owner: *Colonial Williamsburg Foundation. Accession No. 1960 - 316.*

Ball Knop No. 13

Ball Knop No. 14

Ball Knop No. 15

Ball Knop No. 16

Ball Knop No. 17

Ball Knop No. 18
Owner: *Colonial Williamsburg Foundation. Accession No. 1958 - 597.*

Ball Knop No 19

Ball Knop No. 20

Ball Knop No. 21

Supplementary photographs of Ball Knops Nos. 20 and 21.

Ball Knop No. 22
Owner: *Victoria and Albert Museum, London. Accession No. M77 - 1945.*

Ball Knop No. 22
Photo of vestiges of touch mark on flange.
Owner: *Victoria and Albert Museum, London. Accession No. M77 - 1945.*

Ball Knop No. 23

Ball Knop No. 23
Flange marks.

Ball Knop No. 24

Ball Knop No. 24
Photo of touch mark on flange.

Ball Knop No. 25
Owner: *Colonial Williamsburg Foundation. Accession No. 1966 - 297.*

Ball Knop No. 26

Ball Knop No. 27
Owner: *The National Trust Arlington Court. Accession No. CS14.*

Ball Knop No. 28 (left)
Owner: *Colonial Williamsburg Foundation. Accession No. 1961 - 215 (1).*
Ball Knop No. 29 (right)
Owner: *Colonial Williamsburg Foundation. Accession No. 1961 - 215 (2).*

Ball Knop No. 30
Owner: *The Hunterian Museum, Glasgow. Accession No. C 1947.*

Ball Knop No. 30
Photo of seven pointed spindle on underside of nozzle plate.
Owner: *The Hunterian Museum, Glasgow. Accession No. C 1947.*

Ball Knop No. 31
Owner: *Victoria and Albert Museum, London. Accession No. M75 - 1938.*

Ball Knop No. 31
Flange showing trace of touch mark and ownership marks.
Owner: *Victoria and Albert Museum, London. Accession No. M75 - 1938.*

Ball Knop No. 32
Owner: *Art Gallery of New South Wales. Accession No. M12 - 1949.*

Ball Knop No. 33

Ball Knop No. 34

Ball Knop No. 35 (left)
Owner: *Colonial Williamsburg Foundation. Accession No. 1960 - 794 (1).*
Ball Knop No. 36 (right)
Owner: *Colonial Williamsburg Foundation. Accession No. 1960 - 794 (2).*

Ball Knop No. 37

Ball Knop No. 38
Owner: *Victoria and Albert Museum, London. Accession No. M79 - 1945.*

Ball Knop No. 38
Photo showing touch mark on flange of candlestick.
Owner: *Victoria and Albert Museum, London. Accession No. M79 - 1945.*

Ball Knop No. 39
Owner: *Cheltenham Art Gallery and Museum. Accession No. 1976 - 33.*

Ball Knop No. 40

Ball Knop No. 41

Trumpet Based Paten by 'E. Fairbrother 1723'.

Ball Knop Glass c.1700